The Supreme Court

CHRISTINE TAYLOR-BUTLER

Children's Press®
A Division of Scholastic Inc.
New York   Toronto   London   Auckland   Sydney
Mexico City   New Delhi   Hong Kong
Danbury, Connecticut

Content Consultant

David R. Smith, PhD

Academic Adviser and

Adjunct Assistant Professor of History

University of Michigan-Ann Arbor

Reading Consultant

Cecilia Minden-Cupp, PhD

Early Literacy Consultant and Author

Library of Congress Cataloging-in-Publication Data

Taylor-Butler, Christine.
The Supreme Court / by Christine Taylor-Butler.
   p. cm. — (A true book)
Includes bibliographical references and index.
ISBN-13: 978-0-531-12636-3 (lib. bdg.)   978-0-531-14786-3 (pbk.)
ISBN-10: 0-531-12636-6 (lib. bdg.)   0-531-14786-X (pbk.)
1. United States. Supreme Court—History—Juvenile literature. 2.
Courts of last resort—United States—Juvenile literature. 3. Judicial
Process—United States—Juvenile literature. I. Title. II. Series.
KF8742.Z9T39 2007
347.73'26—dc22   2007012257

© 2008 Scholastic Inc.

Find the Truth!

Everything you are about to read is true *except* for one of the sentences on this page.

Which one is **TRUE**?

T or F   Lawyers who present cases before the Supreme Court receive white quill pens.

T or F   Justices serve four-year terms.

Find the answer in this book.

Contents

Today's justices
were appointed by 5
different presidents.

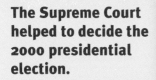

The Supreme Court helped to decide the 2000 presidential election.

THE **BIG** TRUTH!

Justice Stephen Breyer

Justice Clarence Thomas

Justice Ruth Bader Ginsburg

Justice Samuel Alito

Justice Anthony Kennedy

Justice John Paul Stevens

Chief Justice John Roberts Jr.

Justice Antonin Scalia

Justice David Souter

The nine Supreme Court justices pose for a group portrait in 2006.

CHAPTER 1

The Highest Court in the Land

Once appointed, Supreme Court justices can serve for the rest of their lives.

What is the Supreme Court? It is a group of nine judges known as justices. They make sure that the government follows the highest laws of the United States. They ensure every person has access to equal justice under the law. The Supreme Court is the highest court in the land.

THE THREE BRANCHES
OF GOVERNMENT

LEGISLATIVE	UNITED STATES CAPITOL (Home of Congress)	HOUSE OF REPRESENTATIVES SENATE
EXECUTIVE	THE WHITE HOUSE (Home of the President)	PRESIDENT VICE PRESIDENT, CABINET MEMBERS, AND OTHER STAFF
JUDICIAL	SUPREME COURT BUILDING (Home of the Supreme Court)	SUPREME COURT (9 Justices) OTHER FEDERAL COURTS

A handwritten copy of the Constitution is on display at the National Archives in Washington, D.C.

The highest laws are written in the U.S. **Constitution**. Written in 1787, this document was created by the founding fathers to establish the U.S. government. The Constitution divides the government into three parts, or branches. The legislative branch makes the laws. The executive branch carries out the laws. The judicial branch interprets the laws and makes sure they are used and applied fairly.

The judicial branch is made up of all the courts in the **federal**, or national, court system. These courts settle disagreements about what the federal laws mean. There are many levels of courts. Court trials, or **cases**, can begin in the lower courts. Some of those reach the highest one: the Supreme Court.

The Road to the Supreme Court

It is not easy to take a case to the Supreme Court. The process starts when the losing side in a trial decides to try again. They ask a higher court to review the lower court's decision. This is an **appeal**.

THE UNITED STATES FEDERAL COURT SYSTEM

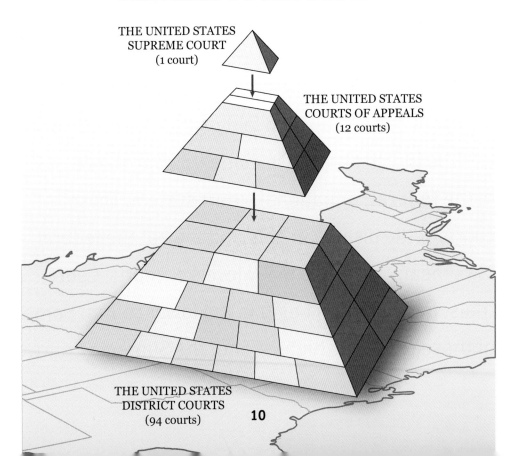

THE UNITED STATES
SUPREME COURT
(1 court)

THE UNITED STATES
COURTS OF APPEALS
(12 courts)

THE UNITED STATES
DISTRICT COURTS
(94 courts)

States have their own supreme courts. Here, the California Supreme Court judges listen to a lawyer present a case.

The higher court has to agree to take the case. Then there is a new trial. If the higher court agrees with the lower court, the losing side can appeal to the next-higher court. Appeals can continue until a case reaches the Supreme Court.

In this way, the judicial branch is shaped like a pyramid. There are many lower courts at the bottom and the Supreme Court at the top. The number of courts where people can try their cases gets smaller as they move up the pyramid.

A cartoon from 1885 depicts Supreme Court justices being overwhelmed with requests to review cases from lower courts.

Each year, the Supreme Court receives thousands of requests from people who want their cases heard. It would be impossible for the justices to take every case. But they do review every request. They hold private meetings before deciding to take a case. Most requests do not make it past this meeting. At least four justices must approve a case before it can be heard.

What types of cases does the Supreme Court take? Some cases involve people or states who disagree over the meaning of a federal law. Other cases concern the Constitution itself. A group's actions might take away another person's rights as explained in the Constitution, for example. The Court also hears cases in which a lower court's ruling goes against an earlier Supreme Court decision. The Supreme Court sometimes uses these cases to fix mistakes made in the past.

The Supreme Court rules on about 100 cases a year — out of about 8,000 requests!

The first U.S. government set up the federal court system. This engraving shows the first president, George Washington (far right), with his advisors in 1789.

CHAPTER 2

Early Days

President George Washington appointed the most Supreme Court justices — 11!

So how does the Supreme Court work? The Constitution created the judicial branch of the U.S. government. But it did not explain how the court system would operate. It also didn't say how many justices the Supreme Court should have. It left the details up to the legislative branch, or the **U.S. Congress**.

Organizing the Lower Courts

In 1789, Congress chose a group of men to set up the federal court system. A Connecticut congressman named Oliver Ellsworth led the group. He wrote the Judiciary Act of 1789. This declared that the Supreme Court would have one chief justice and five associate justices.

The Judiciary Act also set up the lower courts. It grouped the nation's courts into areas called **circuits**. Supreme Court judges traveled along regular routes to hear cases in the circuit courts alongside local judges. It was known as riding circuit.

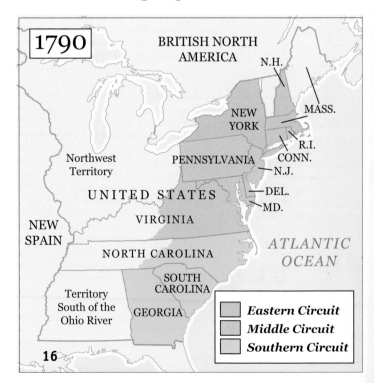

This map shows the federal court circuits in 1790.

1790

BRITISH NORTH AMERICA

N.H.

NEW YORK

MASS.

R.I.
CONN.
N.J.

Northwest Territory

PENNSYLVANIA

DEL.
MD.

UNITED STATES

NEW SPAIN

VIRGINIA

ATLANTIC OCEAN

NORTH CAROLINA

SOUTH CAROLINA

Territory South of the Ohio River

GEORGIA

☐ Eastern Circuit
☐ Middle Circuit
☐ Southern Circuit

U.S. Chief Justices

John Jay
1789–1795

John Rutledge
1795

William Cushing*
1796

Oliver Ellsworth
1796–1800

John Marshall
1801–1835

Roger B. Taney
1836–1864

Salmon P. Chase
1864–1873

Morrison Waite
1874–1888

Melville Fuller
1888–1910

Edward D. White
1910–1921

William H. Taft
1921–1930

Charles E. Hughes
1930–1941

Harlan F. Stone
1941–1946

Fred M. Vinson
1946–1953

Earl Warren
1953–1969

Warren E. Burger
1969–1986

William Rehnquist
1986–2005

John Roberts
2005–present

* He was appointed as chief but did not serve.

The Supreme Court Meets

The Supreme Court met for the first time in New York City in 1790. President George Washington chose a lawyer named John Jay to be chief justice. Jay had helped to write the Constitution.

The first meeting of the Supreme Court did not go as planned. Only three associate justices showed up! The others were too busy or didn't want to make the long trip.

There wasn't much for the justices to do anyway. It took most of the first year to organize the new court system. Judges also spent time riding circuit two times a year. They didn't actually hear any cases until the Supreme Court moved the next year to Philadelphia, Pennsylvania.

Federal appeals courts are still organized into regions called circuits. Today, the United States has 13 circuits.

Stagecoach Justice

Supreme Court justices had to travel from city to city. They spent up to 19 hours a day in bumpy stagecoaches. Roads were often rocky or muddy. The justices complained bitterly about the exhausting travel. Chief Justice John Jay even threatened to quit. In 1793, Congress agreed that justices had to travel to each circuit only once a year instead of twice. No one rides circuit today.

Until smaller courts were established, Supreme Court justices traveled around the country to hear cases.

No Advice Here!

The first Supreme Court set limits on its duties. The justices wanted to keep their powers separate from the other branches of government. They even refused President Washington when he asked for advice.

People were so upset by Jay's Treaty that they burned likenesses of John Jay.

But when Washington asked Chief Justice John Jay to help fix America's poor relationship with the British, Jay agreed. He traveled to Great Britain in 1794 and worked out an agreement called Jay's Treaty. The treaty settled many problems and established peaceful trade policy. Unfortunately, it angered many at home who opposed any agreements with the British. Jay left the Supreme Court the next year to become governor of New York.

Rejected!

The Constitution gives the president the power to choose Supreme Court justices. But the Senate must vote to approve all justices before they formally take their positions. Supreme Court justices usually serve for life, or until they retire.

In 1795, Washington chose Associate Justice John Rutledge to replace John Jay as chief justice. Rutledge complained in public about Jay's Treaty. He said he would rather see President Washington die than agree to sign the treaty! Rutledge's statement shocked many Americans. The Senate rejected Rutledge as chief justice.

John Rutledge served as chief justice for several months before being rejected by the Senate.

John Marshall was the longest serving U.S. Supreme Court chief justice in American history. He served from 1801–1835.

CHAPTER 3

The Marshall Court

John Adams believed that a fitting title for the U.S. president would be "His Majesty the President."

John Adams became president in 1797. In the 1801 election, he lost to his vice president, Thomas Jefferson. One of Adams's last acts as president was selecting John Marshall as chief justice. Marshall would become one of the Court's most famous justices. But that wasn't Adams's only last-minute selection!

President John Adams (right) said appointing John Marshall was "the proudest act of my life."

A Famous Case

On his last night in office, Adams made 48 of his friends federal judges. Thomas Jefferson called these judges "midnight judges." One of these midnight judges was William Marbury.

When he took office, Jefferson ordered his staff, including James Madison, his new secretary of state, not to give Marbury or the others their jobs. Jefferson wanted to appoint his own judges. In 1803, Marbury took his case to the Supreme Court to force Madison to give him the job. This famous case is called *Marbury v. Madison*.

Chief Justice Marshall thought that Marbury deserved the job. But he knew that Jefferson and Madison might simply ignore the Court's decision if they didn't agree with him. That would make the Supreme Court look weak. So Marshall came up with a clever solution.

Marbury v. Madison

Marshall had helped Congress to write the Judiciary Act in 1789. The act allowed the Supreme Court to decide cases such as this one about federal workers. But the U.S. Constitution did not actually grant the Court this power. So Marshall ruled that the Judiciary Act was **unconstitutional**. He announced that the Supreme Court could not hear Marbury's case. Marshall was unable to give Marbury the job he wanted, but he had made the Supreme Court stronger.

Why was Marshall's decision so important? It was the first time the Supreme Court **overruled** a law made by Congress. It confirmed that the Court could rule against laws that don't follow the Constitution. Since then, this power has been an important part of the way our federal government works.

John Marshall served as chief justice until he died in 1835, after a stagecoach accident.

In this painting, Chief Justice John Marshall administers the oath of office to President Andrew Jackson at the U.S. Capitol, on March 4, 1829.

This photo was taken at Thomy Lafon School in New Orleans, Louisiana, in the 1950s. Only African American children attended this school until a Supreme Court ruling outlawed segregation.

CHAPTER 4

Famous Supreme Court Cases

Segregated schools were legal before the Supreme Court found them unconstitutional in 1954.

The justices of the Supreme Court carefully choose the cases they will hear. What kinds of cases do they look for? The Court chooses cases that will have the biggest effect on the rights and freedoms of the greatest number of U.S. citizens. They also choose cases that might allow them to overturn previous decisions.

You're Under Arrest

"You have the right to remain silent. Anything you say can and will be used against you in a court of law." Most people have heard these words on television programs and in movies. Did you know that the Supreme Court is responsible for them?

A 23-year-old man named Ernesto Miranda was arrested and found guilty of kidnapping and other crimes in 1963. He later confessed. But the police never told him about his rights before the confession. The Constitution states that all people have the right to have a lawyer. If a person cannot afford a lawyer, one will be appointed and paid for by the government. People also have the right to not answer police questions if the answers might strengthen the case against them.

Ernesto Miranda (right) speaks to his lawyer. Miranda was later convicted based on witness statements and other evidence.

Police officers often carry a copy of the Miranda rights when they are on duty.

Miranda's case went all the way to the Supreme Court. In the 1966 case called *Miranda v. Arizona,* the Court ruled that police must inform people they arrest of their rights. These are now known as Miranda rights. They include the right to a lawyer and the right to remain silent.

Fixing Mistakes

In the 1857 case called *Dred Scott v. Sandford*, the Supreme Court ruled that African Americans could not become citizens. Congress overruled the Court in 1868. They changed the Constitution to say that any person born on U.S. soil was a citizen.

Dred Scott was a slave who tried unsuccessfully to win his freedom in court.

   A decision called *Plessy v. Ferguson* was also **overturned**. In 1896, the Supreme Court ruled that states could make different races use different, but equally good, public places. This was called **segregation**.

The v. in any court case's name is short for the Latin word *versus,* which means "against."

Often, the public places were not truly equal. African Americans had to ride in the back of buses. African American children went to schools that weren't as good as white children's schools. It took 58 years for the Supreme Court to overturn *Plessy v. Ferguson*. In *Brown v. Board of Education of Topeka*, the justices ruled that separating people based on race was unconstitutional.

This photo is of college students protesting segregation at a Woolworth's store in Greensboro, North Carolina, in 1960. At the time, only white people were allowed to eat at this lunch counter.

Al Gore

George W. Bush

The Court Decides

Bush asks the U.S. Supreme Court to review the Florida court's decision. On December 11, lawyers for both sides in *Bush v. Gore* present their cases before the U.S. Supreme Court. On December 12, the Court announces it has overturned the state court's decision to allow the recount. Gore finally accepts defeat. George W. Bush becomes the 43rd president of the United States.

The Case of the Close Call

For 35 days in 2000, the country held its breath. No one knew who had won the U.S. presidential election. Voting day had long passed, and no winner had been declared. In the end, the Supreme Court had the final word.

Election Day

On November 7, 2000, Americans cast their votes. Which of the two leading candidates will win—George W. Bush or Al Gore?

That Night

The election depends on the vote count in Florida. Bush seems to be ahead. Gore even calls him to offer his congratulations. Then the vote count in Florida begins to change. Then a few hundred votes separate the candidates. Gore calls Bush once again, this time to say he's not admitting defeat.

To Recount or Not to Recount?

Thousands of volunteers in Florida begin recounting paper votes, or ballots, by hand. There is confusion about how to count and which ballots to count. Bush is still slightly ahead of Gore. Bush's team works to stop the recount. On November 21, the Florida Supreme Court decides the recount will continue.

An election worker checks the vote on a ballot.

CHAPTER 5

The Supreme Court Today

Photographers are not allowed to take photos of the Supreme Court when it's in session.

It's 10 A.M. on the first Monday in October. You are inside the courtroom of the Supreme Court building in Washington, D.C. An officer of the court bangs a small wooden mallet called a gavel and cries, "Oyez! Oyez! Oyez!" Everyone in the courtroom rises and stands quietly. The justices enter the chamber and take their places.

This drawing is of an attorney arguing his case in front of the justices in 1974. This hearing concerned the possible impeachment of President Richard Nixon.

You might be wondering what "oyez" (o-YAY) means. It's an old European word meaning "hear ye." It is a Supreme Court tradition to say it at the start of each day in session.

It is a Supreme Court tradition to have quill pens in the courtroom.

The justices follow traditions that began as early as 1789. Each justice wears a black robe to court. White quill pens are always placed on the lawyers' tables as keepsakes.

The Supreme Court meets from October until June or July. This time is divided into two alternating parts—sittings and recesses. Each part lasts about two weeks. Justices hear cases during the "sittings." They do research and write opinions during the "recesses."

Famous Justices

1789
George Washington selects John Jay as the first chief justice.

1801
John Marshall is named chief justice. He holds the office longer than anyone in history—34 years!

In the courtroom, lawyers sit at tables facing the justices. When it is their turn to speak, they stand at a special table called a lectern. There are special seats on the left and right sides of the courtroom. These are for reporters, guests, and other people working on the case.

Ordinary visitors sit on red benches in the back of the courtroom. A court officer hands out two types of tickets. One is for people who want to stay a while. The other one is for people who only want to listen for a few minutes.

1967
Thurgood Marshall becomes the first African American justice.

1981
Sandra Day O'Connor becomes the first female justice.

No sessions are held on Thursdays or Fridays. On those days, the justices meet to discuss cases and to vote on requests from lawyers. The justices must read many cases to decide which ones to take. They have law clerks and **interns** to help them. They also have a very large law library with more than 450,000 books.

Chief Justice William Rehnquist added gold stripes to his robe's sleeves after seeing them in an opera.

William Rehnquist was appointed to the Supreme Court in 1972 and served for 33 years.

HELP WANTED
Supreme Court Intern

In search of responsible college students or recent graduates to work in the Supreme Court. Must have an interest in the law. Interns will prepare daily news summaries and research reports. Some benefits of the position include access to Supreme Court sessions and use of excellent law library. Also includes lunch meetings with justices. Salary: None

If interested, send résumé, transcript, and letters of recommendation to www.supremecourtus.gov. Include an essay on the importance of the U.S. Constitution.

The Modern Court

The justices of the Supreme Court promise to defend, or uphold, the Constitution. They carefully balance the rights of people with the rights of the state and federal governments. They make sure the laws of the Constitution are used fairly. After more than 200 years, the Supreme Court of the United States remains one of the most important and respected courts in the world. ★

During Court sessions, the Chief Justice sits in the center. The newest justices sit at the ends of the row.

Court created by: the U.S. Constitution

Justices are appointed by: The U.S. president, with approval by the Senate

Supreme Court's first session on: February 2, 1790

Number of justices when Supreme Court began: 6

Number of justices today: 9

First chief justice: John Jay

First location of the Supreme Court: New York City

Current location of the Supreme Court: Washington, D.C.

Youngest justice: Joseph Story, age 32

Oldest justice appointed: Horace Lurton, age 65

Did you find the truth?

T Lawyers who present cases before the Supreme Court receive white quill pens.

F Justices serve four-year terms.

Resources

Books

Giddens-White, Bryon. *The Supreme Court and the Judicial Branch*. Chicago: Heinemann Library, 2005.

January, Brendan. *The Supreme Court*. Danbury, CT: Franklin Watts, 2005.

Landau, Elaine. *The 2000 Presidential Election*. Danbury, CT: Children's Press, 2002.

Murphy, Patricia J. *The U.S. Supreme Court*. Minneapolis: Compass Point Books, 2002.

Panchyk, Richard. *Our Supreme Court: A History with 14 Activities*. Chicago: Chicago Review Press, Inc., 2006.

Taylor-Butler, Christine. *The Bill of Rights*. Danbury, CT: Children's Press, 2007.

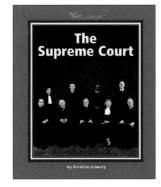

Organizations and Web Sites

**Court TV Online—The Supreme Court:
A Journey Through Time**

www.courttv.com/archive/multimedia/supremecourt/
View a multimedia presentation on the Supreme Court.

The Supreme Court Historical Society

www.supremecourthistory.org
Check out information about the Supreme Court's
fascinating history.

U.S. Courts—Educational Outreach

www.uscourts.gov/outreach/resources/homeworkhelp.html
Visit this site for easy-to-use graphs, charts, games, and other
resources for students.

Places to Visit

**The Supreme Court of the
United States**
One First Street, NE
Washington, DC 20543
202-479-3211
www.supremecourtus.gov
See the real-life Supreme
Court in session.

Important Words

appeal – a legal process in which the losing side asks a higher court to review a lower court's decision

ballots (BA-luhts) – pieces of paper on which a voter marks a choice

cases – lawsuits or legal actions brought to court

circuits (SUR-kits) – regular routes followed by a traveling judge

Constitution (kon-stuh-TOO-shun) – the 1787 document that explains the people's rights and the U.S. government's powers

federal – relating to a form of government in which states are united under one central power

interns – people who are learning a skill or a job by working with an expert

overruled – declared to be wrong and in need of correction

overturned – reversed a decision that someone else made

segregation – the act of setting apart one group of people from another

unconstitutional (uhn-KON-stuh-TOO-shuh-nuhl) – not keeping with the basic laws set forth by the Constitution

U.S. Congress – the legislative branch of government, made up of the Senate and the House of Representatives

Index

About the Author

Christine Taylor-Butler has written more than 30 books for children. She has written several books in the True Book American History series, including *The Bill of Rights*, *The Constitution*, *The Congress of the United States*, and *The Presidency*.

A native of Ohio, Taylor-Butler now lives in Kansas City, Missouri, with her husband, Ken, and their two daughters. She holds degrees in both civil engineering and art and design from the Massachusetts Institute of Technology.